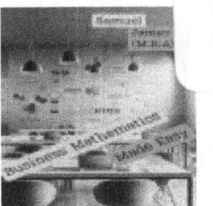

Business Mathematics Made Easy

Dr. Samuel James MBA

Published by Samuel Inbaraja S, 2024.

Business Mathematics Made Easy

Samuel James

Contents

Chapter 1: Fundamentals of Business Mathematics 1
Chapter 2: Profit and Loss Analysis 4
Chapter 3: Interest Calculations 7
Chapter 4: Financial Statements and Ratios 10
Chapter 5: Budgeting and Forecasting 14
Chapter 6: Pricing Strategies 16
Chapter 7: Break-Even Analysis 19
Chapter 8: Inventory Management 22
Chapter 9: Marketing Metrics 25
Chapter 10: Time Value of Money 28
Chapter 11: Risk Assessment and Management 30
Chapter 12: Annuities and Amortization 33
Chapter 13: Advanced Statistical Methods in Business 36
Conclusion: How to Use AI for Business Math 38

Chapter 1: Fundamentals of Business Mathematics

Overview of Key Concepts

Business mathematics is an essential tool for solving real-world business problems. It involves applying mathematical techniques to help in decision-making processes in finance, marketing, operations, and more. In this chapter, we will explore basic mathematical principles that form the foundation of business math.

Question to Ponder:

What areas of business do you think rely most on mathematics? Write down a few examples before continuing.

Basic Mathematical Principles in Business

Let's start with some fundamental concepts that are used frequently in business settings:

1. **Addition and Subtraction** – Used in budgeting, profit and loss calculations, and financial forecasting.
2. **Multiplication and Division** – Essential for scaling business models, pricing products, and calculating revenue growth.
3. **Percentages** – Useful in calculating discounts, interest rates, and profit margins.
4. **Ratios and Proportions** – Key to understanding financial health and comparing different business metrics.

Question for Reflection:

How often do you use percentages in your day-to-day activities? Can you recall an instance when you had to calculate a percentage?

Practical Example:

Imagine you own a small business that sells electronics. If you sold $1,000 worth of products last week and had to give a 10% discount on a few items, how would you calculate the total discount given?

Basic Mathematical Operations in Business Contexts

1. **Cost Calculation**:
   Let's say you're running a retail shop. You purchase a product for $500 and want to sell it at a 20% markup. The formula to calculate the selling price would be:
   $$\text{Selling Price} = \text{Cost Price} + (\text{Cost Price} \times \text{Markup Percentage})$$
   Using the formula:
   $$\text{Selling Price} = 500 + (500 \times 0.20) = 600$$
   So, you would sell the product for $600.

Challenge Question:

If you were to offer a 5% discount on that $600 item, how would you calculate the final price?

Key Takeaways

- Basic mathematical principles, like addition, subtraction, multiplication, and division, are the building blocks of business decisions.
- Percentages and ratios are widely used in pricing, financial analysis, and performance metrics.

Discussion Prompt:

Think about your own business or an imaginary one. What kind of calculations do you think you'd be doing on a regular basis?

Challenge Question Answer from Chapter 1:

If you were to offer a 5% discount on the $600 item, the calculation would be as follows:

1. First, calculate the discount:
   Discount=600×0.05=30\text{Discount} = 600 \times 0.05 = 30Discount=600×0.05=30
2. Subtract the discount from the selling price:
   Final Price=600−30=570\text{Final Price} = 600 - 30 = 570Final Price=600−30=570

So, the final price after a 5% discount would be **$570**.

Chapter 2: Profit and Loss Analysis

Understanding Profit Margins

Profit margins are crucial for determining how much money a business earns from its sales after deducting all the expenses. There are two main types of profit margins: **gross profit margin** and **net profit margin**.

- **Gross Profit Margin** is calculated as:
  $$\text{Gross Profit Margin} = \frac{\text{Revenue} - \text{Cost of Goods Sold (COGS)}}{\text{Revenue}} \times 100$$
- **Net Profit Margin** is calculated as:
  $$\text{Net Profit Margin} = \frac{\text{Net Income}}{\text{Revenue}} \times 100$$

Question to Ponder:

What's the difference between gross profit and net profit? Can you think of an expense that might be included in net profit but not in gross profit?

Case Study: Profit Calculation for a Retail Business

Let's apply this to a real-world example. Suppose a retail business has the following data:

- Total sales revenue for the month: $50,000
- Cost of Goods Sold (COGS): $30,000

- Operating expenses: $10,000

Step 1: Calculate Gross Profit

Gross Profit = Revenue - COGS

$$\text{Gross Profit} = 50,000 - 30,000 = 20,000$$

Step 2: Calculate Gross Profit Margin

$$\text{Gross Profit Margin} = \frac{20,000}{50,000} \times 100 = 40\%$$

Step 3: Calculate Net Profit

Net Profit = Gross Profit - Operating Expenses

$$\text{Net Profit} = 20,000 - 10,000 = 10,000$$

Step 4: Calculate Net Profit Margin

$$\text{Net Profit Margin} = \frac{10,000}{50,000} \times 100 = 20\%$$

Challenge Question:

If the business wanted to increase its net profit margin to 25%, what would need to change—revenues, expenses, or COGS? How could the business make this happen?

Key Takeaways

- Profit margins provide valuable insight into a company's profitability.
- Gross profit margin only considers direct costs (COGS), while net profit margin includes all expenses.

Discussion Prompt:

Think about a product or service you're familiar with. How do you think the company behind it manages its costs and profit margins? What steps could they take to increase profitability?

Chapter 3: Interest Calculations

Simple vs. Compound Interest

Interest is the cost of borrowing money or the return on an investment. There are two main types:

- **Simple Interest**: Calculated only on the original principal amount.
  Formula:
  $$\text{Simple Interest} = P \times r \times t$$
  where P is the principal, r is the interest rate, and t is time.
- **Compound Interest**: Calculated on the initial principal and also on the accumulated interest from previous periods.
  Formula:
  $$\text{Compound Interest} = P \times \left(1 + \frac{r}{n}\right)^{nt}$$
  where n is the number of times the interest is compounded per year.

Question to Reflect:

Why would a borrower prefer simple interest over compound interest? Can you think of any cases where compound interest might be more beneficial to the borrower?

Case Study: Loan Repayment Scenarios

Consider a loan of $5,000 with an interest rate of 5% per year for 3 years.

Scenario 1: Simple Interest

Using the formula for simple interest:

Simple Interest = $5{,}000 \times 0.05 \times 3 = 750$

Total repayment = Principal + Interest = $5,000 + $750 = **$5,750**

Scenario 2: Compound Interest (compounded annually)

Using the compound interest formula:

Compound Interest = $5{,}000 \times (1+0.05)^3 = 5{,}000 \times 1.157625 = 5{,}788.13$

So, the total repayment would be **$5,788.13**.

Challenge Question:

If the compound interest was compounded quarterly, how would that affect the total repayment? Try calculating it using the formula provided.

Key Takeaways

- Simple interest is easier to calculate and typically results in lower repayment amounts.
- Compound interest grows faster over time, making it more expensive for borrowers but more beneficial for investors.

Discussion Prompt:

What kind of loans or investments might use compound interest? How do you think the frequency of compounding (monthly, quarterly, etc.) impacts the total cost?

Use Generative AI like Google Gemini or ChatGPT for discuss and learn.

Chapter 4: Financial Statements and Ratios

Key Financial Statements Overview

Financial statements are essential tools for understanding the financial health of a business. There are three key financial statements every business should prepare:

1. **Income Statement** (also known as the Profit and Loss Statement): Shows the company's revenues, costs, and profit over a period of time.
2. **Balance Sheet**: Provides a snapshot of the company's assets, liabilities, and equity at a specific point in time.
3. **Cash Flow Statement**: Tracks the cash inflows and outflows over a period of time, divided into operating, investing, and financing activities.

Question to Ponder:

Can you think of a situation where a business could be profitable on its income statement but still face cash flow problems? What might cause that?

Case Study: Ratio Analysis for Decision Making

Financial ratios are powerful tools that help businesses and investors analyze financial statements. Let's explore some key ratios using the financial data of a fictitious company, **ABC Corp**:

ABC Corp's Financial Data:

- Revenue: $500,000
- Net Income: $50,000

- Total Assets: $250,000
- Total Liabilities: $150,000

Step 1: Calculate the Profit Margin

The profit margin measures how much profit a company makes for each dollar of sales.

Formula:

$$\text{Profit Margin} = \frac{\text{Net Income}}{\text{Revenue}} \times 100$$

Calculation:

$$\text{Profit Margin} = \frac{50{,}000}{500{,}000} \times 100 = 10\%$$

This means ABC Corp earns 10 cents of profit for every dollar of revenue.

Step 2: Calculate the Return on Assets (ROA)

ROA measures how effectively a company is using its assets to generate profit.

Formula:

$$\text{ROA} = \frac{\text{Net Income}}{\text{Total Assets}} \times 100$$

Calculation:

$$\text{ROA} = \frac{50{,}000}{250{,}000} \times 100 = 20\%$$

ABC Corp is generating 20% returns on its assets.

Step 3: Calculate the Debt-to-Equity Ratio

This ratio shows the proportion of company financing that comes from debt and equity.

Formula:

$$\text{Debt-to-Equity Ratio} = \frac{\text{Total Liabilities}}{\text{Total Equity}}$$

First, calculate the equity:

$$\text{Total Equity} = \text{Total Assets} - \text{Total Liabilities} = 250{,}000 - 150{,}000 = 100{,}000$$

Now, calculate the ratio:

$$\text{Debt-to-Equity Ratio} = \frac{150{,}000}{100{,}000} = 1.5$$

This means that for every dollar of equity, the company has $1.50 of debt.

Challenge Question:

If ABC Corp wanted to lower its debt-to-equity ratio, what strategies could it pursue? Would increasing assets or paying off liabilities be more effective?

Key Takeaways

- Financial ratios give insights into a company's profitability, efficiency, and financial structure.
- Ratios like profit margin, ROA, and debt-to-equity can help in making strategic business decisions.

Discussion Prompt:

Think about a business you're familiar with. How do you think financial ratios could help that business identify areas for improvement?

Chapter 5: Budgeting and Forecasting

Importance of Budgeting in Business

Budgeting is a crucial activity that helps businesses plan for the future by allocating resources effectively. It involves predicting future revenues, costs, and expenses to ensure the business remains on track financially.

There are several types of budgets, such as:

- **Operating Budget**: Focuses on income and expenses related to daily operations.
- **Cash Flow Budget**: Forecasts cash inflows and outflows over a specific period.
- **Capital Budget**: Plans for long-term investments, like purchasing equipment or facilities.

Question to Reflect:

Why might a business need different types of budgets for operations, cash flow, and capital projects? Can you think of an example for each?

Case Study: Developing a Budget for a Startup

Imagine you're starting a small business selling handmade crafts. You expect to sell 1,000 items in the first year at an average price of $20 per item. You estimate your total costs for materials, marketing, and other expenses to be $15,000.

Step 1: Estimate Revenue

Revenue = Price per item × Number of items sold

$$\text{Revenue} = 20 \times 1{,}000 = 20{,}000$$

Step 2: Estimate Costs

Estimated total costs = $15,000

Step 3: Calculate Profit

Profit = Revenue - Costs

$$\text{Profit} = 20{,}000 - 15{,}000 = 5{,}000$$

Now, based on this budget, you have a predicted profit of $5,000 for the first year.

Challenge Question:

If you want to increase your profit margin by 10%, what actions could you take to adjust your budget? Consider both revenue and cost changes.

Key Takeaways

- Budgeting helps businesses predict and control their financial future.
- A well-prepared budget can highlight areas where costs might be too high or revenues could be improved.

Discussion Prompt:

Consider a startup idea you have or one you know. How would you go about creating a budget for it? What factors would you need to consider to ensure success?

Chapter 6: Pricing Strategies

Factors Influencing Pricing Decisions

Pricing is one of the most important decisions a business can make. A well-thought-out pricing strategy can drive sales, improve profitability, and even shape the perception of a brand. Several factors influence pricing decisions, including:

1. **Cost of Production**: The total cost to produce a product, including materials, labor, and overhead.
2. **Market Demand**: Higher demand can lead to higher prices, while lower demand may force a reduction in price.
3. **Competition**: Competitors' prices often dictate how much you can charge for similar products.
4. **Customer Perception**: Premium pricing can create the perception of high quality, while discount pricing can attract bargain hunters.
5. **Economic Conditions**: Inflation, interest rates, and overall economic health impact how much consumers are willing to spend.

Question to Ponder:

How do you think pricing decisions might differ between luxury products and budget products? What factors would be most important for each?

Case Study: Pricing Strategy for a New Product Launch

Imagine you are launching a new organic skincare product line. You need to decide on the price for your products. Here's some information to guide your decision:

- **Production Costs**: $15 per product.
- **Competitor Pricing**: Competitors sell similar organic skincare products for between $30 and $40.
- **Target Market**: Consumers looking for natural, eco-friendly skincare solutions.
- **Marketing and Branding Costs**: You've invested heavily in branding your product as premium and eco-friendly.

Step 1: Determine Your Pricing Objective

Is your goal to maximize profits, gain market share, or build a premium brand image? Since you've invested in branding, let's aim for a premium pricing strategy to build your brand.

Step 2: Set the Price

Given your production cost of $15 and competitor prices, you might consider pricing your product at $35 to position it as high-quality but still within the competitive range.

Step 3: Monitor Market Response

After launching, you'll need to keep an eye on customer response. If sales are slow, you might consider offering promotions or adjusting the price.

Challenge Question:

If your sales start off slower than expected, should you lower your price immediately, or are there other strategies you could try to boost sales without cutting into your premium image?

Key Takeaways

- Pricing strategies must balance cost, competition, and customer perception.
- Premium pricing can boost brand image, but it's crucial to deliver value that justifies the higher cost.

Discussion Prompt:

Think of a product you've purchased recently. How do you think the company arrived at the price? What factors do you believe influenced their pricing decision?

Chapter 7: Break-Even Analysis

Understanding Break-Even Points

The break-even point is the level of sales at which a company neither makes a profit nor incurs a loss. It's an essential concept for businesses, especially when launching new products or services. Knowing your break-even point helps you understand how much you need to sell to cover your costs.

The formula to calculate the break-even point in units is:

$$\text{Break-Even Point (units)} = \frac{\text{Fixed Costs}}{\text{Selling Price per Unit} - \text{Variable Cost per Unit}}$$

- **Fixed Costs**: Costs that don't change with production (e.g., rent, salaries).
- **Variable Costs**: Costs that vary with production (e.g., materials, labor).
- **Selling Price per Unit**: The price at which you sell each product.

Question to Reflect:

Why is it important to know your break-even point before launching a new product? How might it affect your pricing or sales strategies?

Case Study: Break-Even Analysis for a Service Business

Imagine you run a graphic design service and charge $200 per project. Your fixed monthly costs are $1,000 (e.g., office rent, software subscriptions), and your variable costs (e.g., printing, materials) are $50 per project.

Step 1: Identify Costs

- Fixed Costs = $1,000
- Variable Costs per project = $50
- Selling Price per project = $200

Step 2: Calculate the Break-Even Point

Using the formula:

$$\text{Break-Even Point (projects)} = \frac{1{,}000}{200 - 50} = \frac{1{,}000}{150} \approx 6.67$$

So, you need to complete **7 projects** in a month to break even.

Step 3: Adjust for Profit

If you want to make a profit, you'll need to complete more than 7 projects. For example, if you want a monthly profit of $1,000, you'd need to complete:

$$\frac{1{,}000 + 1{,}000}{150} \approx 13.33$$

That means you'd need to complete 14 projects to reach your profit goal.

Challenge Question:

If you raised your price to $250 per project, how would that affect your break-even point? Would it reduce the number of projects you need to complete, and by how much?

Key Takeaways

- Break-even analysis is crucial for determining how many sales you need to cover your costs.
- Understanding your break-even point can help set realistic sales goals and pricing strategies.

Discussion Prompt:

Think about a service you've used recently. How many customers do you think the service provider needs to break even? How might their fixed and variable costs affect their pricing decisions?

Chapter 8: Inventory Management

Mathematical Models for Inventory Control

Effective inventory management ensures that a business has the right amount of stock available to meet customer demand without overstocking, which ties up cash, or understocking, which can lead to lost sales. Several mathematical models help businesses determine optimal inventory levels:

1. **Economic Order Quantity (EOQ)**: This model calculates the optimal order quantity that minimizes total inventory costs, including ordering and holding costs.
   Formula:
   $$EOQ = \sqrt{\frac{2DS}{H}}$$
   Where:
   - D = demand in units
   - S = ordering cost per order
   - H = holding cost per unit per year
2. **Reorder Point (ROP)**: This tells a business when to place a new order to avoid running out of stock.
   Formula:
   $$ROP = \text{Lead Time Demand}$$
   Where:
   - *Lead Time Demand* = average daily usage × lead time in days.

Question to Reflect:

Why is it important for businesses to balance between holding too much and too little inventory? Can you think of any industries where inventory management is especially critical?

Case Study: Inventory Turnover Analysis in Retail

Inventory turnover is a ratio that shows how often a company sells and replaces its inventory over a period. A high turnover rate may indicate strong sales, while a low turnover rate can suggest overstocking.

ABC Retail has the following information for the year:

- **Cost of Goods Sold (COGS)**: $500,000
- **Average Inventory**: $100,000

Step 1: Calculate Inventory Turnover

Inventory turnover is calculated using the following formula:

$$\text{Inventory Turnover} = \frac{\text{COGS}}{\text{Average Inventory}}$$

Using the values from ABC Retail:

$$\text{Inventory Turnover} = \frac{500{,}000}{100{,}000} = 5$$

This means ABC Retail sells and replaces its inventory 5 times a year.

Step 2: Calculate Days in Inventory

Days in inventory indicates how long, on average, it takes for a company to sell its inventory. It's calculated as:

$$\text{Days in Inventory} = \frac{365}{\text{Inventory Turnover}}$$

For ABC Retail:

$$\text{Days in Inventory} = \frac{365}{5} = 73$$

So, on average, it takes 73 days for ABC Retail to sell its entire inventory.

Challenge Question:

If ABC Retail wanted to increase its inventory turnover to 6, what would need to happen—should it increase sales, decrease inventory, or both? What strategies might help achieve this?

Key Takeaways

- Inventory management is crucial for controlling costs and ensuring customer satisfaction.
- Ratios like inventory turnover help businesses understand how efficiently they are managing their stock.

Discussion Prompt:

Think of a company that relies heavily on inventory, such as a grocery store or an electronics retailer. How do you think they balance having enough stock without overstocking? How might seasonality affect their inventory management decisions?

Chapter 9: Marketing Metrics

Key Metrics for Marketing Performance

Marketing metrics help businesses evaluate the effectiveness of their marketing efforts. Some of the most important metrics include:

1. **Customer Acquisition Cost (CAC)**: The cost of acquiring a new customer.
   Formula:
   $$\text{CAC} = \frac{\text{Total Sales and Marketing Costs}}{\text{Number of New Customers Acquired}}$$

2. **Customer Lifetime Value (CLV)**: The total revenue a business expects to earn from a customer over their lifetime.
   Formula:
   $$\text{CLV} = \text{Average Purchase Value} \times \text{Number of Purchases per Year} \times \text{Customer Lifespan}$$

3. **Return on Marketing Investment (ROMI)**: The return generated from marketing activities.
   Formula:
   $$\text{ROMI} = \frac{\text{Revenue Attributed to Marketing}}{\text{Marketing Costs}} \times 100$$

Question to Reflect:

Why might a business with a low customer acquisition cost still struggle with profitability? What role does customer lifetime value play in long-term success?

Case Study: Analyzing Marketing ROI

Consider **XYZ Corp**, a company that has spent $50,000 on a new marketing campaign. From this campaign, they acquired 500 new customers, each of whom is expected to generate $300 in revenue over the next year.

Step 1: Calculate Customer Acquisition Cost (CAC)

Using the formula:

$$CAC = \frac{50{,}000}{500} = 100$$

XYZ Corp's CAC is $100 per new customer.

Step 2: Calculate Customer Lifetime Value (CLV)

If the average customer makes 5 purchases per year, and each purchase is worth $60, we can calculate CLV as:

$$CLV = 60 \times 5 \times 1 = 300$$

So, each customer generates $300 in revenue over the next year.

Step 3: Calculate Return on Marketing Investment (ROMI)

Using the formula:

$$ROMI = \frac{300 \times 500}{50{,}000} \times 100 = 300\%$$

XYZ Corp's ROMI is 300%, meaning they generated $3 in revenue for every $1 spent on marketing.

Challenge Question:

If XYZ Corp wanted to reduce its CAC, what marketing strategies could it employ? Should they focus on improving marketing efficiency or increasing customer retention?

Key Takeaways

- Marketing metrics provide valuable insights into how efficiently a company is spending its marketing budget.
- Understanding metrics like CAC and CLV helps businesses make informed decisions about their marketing strategies.

Discussion Prompt:

Think about the last marketing campaign that influenced you to buy something. How do you think the company calculated the success of that campaign? What metrics might they have used?

Chapter 10: Time Value of Money

Concepts of Present and Future Value

The concept of the time value of money (TVM) is fundamental in finance. It's based on the idea that a dollar today is worth more than a dollar in the future due to its potential earning capacity. This principle can be used to calculate two key concepts:

1. **Present Value (PV)**: The current value of a future sum of money.
   Formula:
   $PV = \frac{FV}{(1+r)^t}$
   Where:
   - FV = future value
   - r = interest rate (as a decimal)
   - t = time in years.
2. **Future Value (FV)**: The value of a current sum of money at a future date, based on a certain interest rate.
   Formula:
   $FV = PV \times (1+r)^t$

Question to Ponder:

Why would an investor prefer to receive money today rather than in the future? How does inflation play a role in this decision?

Case Study: Investment Decisions Based on Time Value

Let's consider an investment decision. You have the option to receive $10,000 today or $11,000 one year from now. The interest rate is 5%. Which option is better?

Step 1: Calculate the Present Value of $11,000

Using the PV formula:

$$PV = \frac{11{,}000}{(1+0.05)^1} = \frac{11{,}000}{1.05} \approx 10{,}476.19$$

This means that $11,000 received one year from now is worth approximately $10,476.19 today.

Step 2: Compare the Two Options

- Option 1: $10,000 today
- Option 2: Present value of $11,000 in one year = $10,476.19

Since $10,476.19 is greater than $10,000, you should choose the future payment of $11,000 in one year.

Challenge Question:

What if the interest rate was 8% instead of 5%? Would that change your decision? Try recalculating the present value of $11,000 with the new interest rate.

Key Takeaways

- The time value of money helps you decide whether to take a payment today or wait for a larger payment in the future.
- Present and future value calculations are essential for making sound financial decisions, especially in investments and loans.

Discussion Prompt:

Think of a financial decision you've made or are considering (buying a car, taking out a loan, etc.). How could the time value of money help you make a better decision?

Chapter 11: Risk Assessment and Management

Quantitative Approaches to Risk Management

In business, managing risk is crucial to success. Quantitative risk management involves using statistical methods to assess the likelihood of different outcomes and their impact on a business.

Some common approaches include:

1. **Expected Value (EV)**: This calculates the average outcome of a decision based on all possible outcomes and their probabilities.
   Formula:
   $$EV = \sum (\text{Probability of Outcome} \times \text{Value of Outcome})$$
2. **Standard Deviation**: This measures the volatility of returns. A higher standard deviation indicates greater risk.
3. **Scenario Analysis**: This involves evaluating the best, worst, and most likely outcomes of a decision.

Question to Reflect:

Why might a company with a higher risk tolerance be willing to pursue investments with a high standard deviation? What kind of business might prefer lower-risk, stable investments?

Case Study: Risk Analysis in Project Management

Imagine you are managing a construction project with the following potential outcomes:

- **Best-case scenario**: A profit of $200,000 (30% probability)
- **Most-likely scenario**: A profit of $150,000 (50% probability)
- **Worst-case scenario**: A profit of $50,000 (20% probability)

Step 1: Calculate the Expected Value

Using the expected value formula:

$$EV = (0.30 \times 200{,}000) + (0.50 \times 150{,}000) + (0.20 \times 50{,}000)$$

$$EV = 60{,}000 + 75{,}000 + 10{,}000 = 145{,}000$$

The expected profit for the project is $145,000.

Step 2: Evaluate Risk

Now, consider how much risk you're willing to take. Although the most likely scenario is $150,000, there's a 20% chance you'll only earn $50,000. Is that risk acceptable, or should you adjust the project plan to reduce potential losses?

Challenge Question:

What strategies could you use to mitigate the risk of earning only $50,000? Could you negotiate better contracts, reduce costs, or build in contingency plans?

Key Takeaways

- Quantitative risk management helps businesses make informed decisions by assessing the potential risks and rewards of various outcomes.
- Tools like expected value and scenario analysis provide a clearer picture of possible risks.

Discussion Prompt:

Think about a project or investment you've been part of or heard about. How did the decision-makers assess the risks involved? What tools or methods could they have used to manage those risks more effectively?

Chapter 12: Annuities and Amortization

Understanding Annuities and Their Applications

An annuity is a series of equal payments made at regular intervals over a specified period of time. Annuities are commonly used for investments, loans, and retirement plans. There are two types of annuities:

1. **Ordinary Annuity**: Payments are made at the end of each period (e.g., monthly or yearly).
   Formula to calculate the present value of an ordinary annuity:
   $$PV = P \times \left(\frac{1 - (1 + r)^{-n}}{r} \right)$$
   Where:
   - P = payment per period
   - r = interest rate per period
   - n = number of periods.
2. **Annuity Due**: Payments are made at the beginning of each period. The formulas are similar to those for ordinary annuities but are adjusted slightly for the timing of payments.

Question to Ponder:

Why do you think an investor would prefer an annuity due over an ordinary annuity? How does receiving payments at the start of each period impact the overall value of the annuity?

Case Study: Amortization Schedule for a Mortgage

Amortization is the process of paying off a loan over time through regular payments. Each payment covers both the interest on the loan and a portion of the principal.

Let's say you've taken out a $200,000 mortgage with a 5% annual interest rate, and you plan to repay it over 30 years with monthly payments. How would you calculate your monthly payment and create an amortization schedule?

Step 1: Calculate the Monthly Payment

Using the annuity formula for loan payments:

$$P = \frac{r \times PV}{1 - (1 + r)^{-n}}$$

Where:

- PV = loan amount = $200,000
- r = monthly interest rate = $\frac{0.05}{12} = 0.004167$
- n = total number of payments = $30 \times 12 = 360$

Plugging in the values:

$$P = \frac{0.004167 \times 200,000}{1 - (1 + 0.004167)^{-360}}$$

$$P \approx 1,073.64$$

So, your monthly mortgage payment is approximately **$1,073.64**.

Step 2: Create the Amortization Schedule

Each payment reduces the loan principal while covering the interest. Initially, a larger portion of the payment goes toward interest, but over time, more goes toward the principal.

For example, in the first month:

- Interest for the first month = $200,000 × 0.004167 = $833.33
- Payment toward principal = $1,073.64 - $833.33 = $240.31
- Remaining loan balance = $200,000 - $240.31 = $199,759.69

This process continues each month until the loan is fully paid off.

Challenge Question:

How would the monthly payment and total interest paid over the life of the loan change if the interest rate increased to 6%? Try recalculating the monthly payment with the new interest rate.

Key Takeaways

- Annuities provide regular payments over time and are commonly used for loans, investments, and retirement plans.
- Amortization schedules help borrowers understand how their payments are applied to the loan's principal and interest over time.

Discussion Prompt:

Think about a loan or investment you've had (or might have in the future). How does understanding amortization help you make better financial decisions? What factors would you consider when choosing between different loan options?

Chapter 13: Advanced Statistical Methods in Business

Application of Statistics in Decision Making

Statistics play a critical role in business decision-making by providing insights based on data analysis. Some advanced statistical methods include:

1. **Regression Analysis**: A statistical technique used to understand the relationship between dependent and independent variables. For example, predicting sales based on advertising expenditure.
2. **Hypothesis Testing**: A process for making decisions based on data. It helps in testing assumptions or claims, like whether a new marketing campaign is more effective than the previous one.
3. **Time Series Analysis**: Used to analyze data points collected over time, such as stock prices or monthly sales, to identify trends and make predictions.

Question to Reflect:

How might a business use regression analysis to forecast future sales? What other factors, beyond advertising, could be included in such a model to improve its accuracy?

Case Study: Using Statistical Analysis for Market Research

Imagine you are conducting market research to determine which factors influence customer satisfaction at a restaurant chain. You collect data on the following variables:

- **Service quality** (scale of 1-10)

- **Food quality** (scale of 1-10)
- **Price** (total spent per customer)
- **Customer satisfaction** (scale of 1-10)

Step 1: Perform Regression Analysis

You want to see how service quality, food quality, and price impact customer satisfaction. The result might show that service quality has the strongest correlation with satisfaction, followed by food quality and price.

Step 2: Interpret the Results

Based on your findings, you might recommend that the restaurant focus on improving service and food quality to boost customer satisfaction, as price appears to have a lesser impact.

Challenge Question:

If food quality has a stronger impact on customer satisfaction than service quality, what steps might the restaurant take to improve its menu or ingredients? How could statistical methods help track the effectiveness of these changes?

Key Takeaways

- Advanced statistical methods help businesses analyze data and make informed decisions.
- Techniques like regression analysis and time series analysis provide insights into patterns, trends, and relationships between variables.

Discussion Prompt:

Think about a business that relies on data analysis to improve its performance. How do you think they use statistical methods to make decisions? What data do you think they prioritize in their analyses?

Conclusion: How to Use AI for Business Math

Advantages of Using AI in Business Mathematics

Artificial Intelligence (AI) has revolutionized various fields, and business mathematics is no exception. AI can significantly improve the accuracy, speed, and efficiency of mathematical calculations and analyses, making it a powerful tool for businesses. Let's explore some key advantages of integrating AI into business math:

1. **Enhanced Data Analysis**
   AI-powered tools can analyze vast amounts of data quickly and efficiently, providing businesses with insights that would be difficult to achieve manually. For example, AI can spot trends in financial data, predict future outcomes, and help businesses make data-driven decisions.
2. **Automating Repetitive Tasks**
   Many mathematical tasks in business, like creating financial statements, calculating interest, or conducting profit and loss analysis, can be automated using AI. This saves time and reduces the risk of human error.
3. **Improved Accuracy and Precision**
   AI systems excel at performing complex mathematical calculations with a high level of precision. This is especially useful in areas like risk assessment, forecasting, and inventory management, where even small errors can have significant consequences.
4. **Real-Time Monitoring and Decision Making**
   AI can monitor real-time data, such as stock levels, sales patterns, and market trends. This allows businesses to make adjustments on the fly, optimizing pricing strategies, inventory control, and marketing efforts instantly based on up-to-date information.

5. **Predictive Analytics**
   By leveraging AI for predictive analytics, businesses can forecast future trends with greater accuracy. This is particularly useful for financial forecasting, demand planning, and understanding customer behavior.

Question to Ponder:

How might AI change the way businesses handle their financial planning and forecasting? Could the use of AI allow businesses to make more proactive decisions rather than reactive ones?

Creating a Significant Impact Using AI in Business Math

To create a significant impact using AI in business math, companies should focus on the following strategies:

1. **Incorporating AI into Financial Modeling**
   Businesses can use AI to build complex financial models that consider various factors, from market trends to internal performance indicators. AI can help with scenario analysis, allowing businesses to predict how changes in one area (e.g., raw material costs) will affect profitability, cash flow, and other financial metrics.
2. **AI-Powered Inventory Management**
   In inventory management, AI can optimize stock levels by analyzing historical sales data and predicting future demand. This minimizes the risk of overstocking or running out of stock, which can lead to financial losses. For example, AI can suggest the best times to reorder products based on trends in customer demand, ensuring a more efficient supply chain.
3. **AI in Pricing Strategy Optimization**
   AI can analyze consumer behavior, competitor pricing, and market conditions in real-time to help businesses determine the optimal pricing for their products. Dynamic pricing models powered by AI allow businesses to adjust prices in response to changes in demand, maximizing revenue and profit.

4. **AI-Assisted Risk Management**
   In risk management, AI can analyze potential risks in investment portfolios, market fluctuations, or supply chain vulnerabilities. It can quickly process vast amounts of data and simulate various scenarios, providing businesses with a clear understanding of potential risks and strategies to mitigate them.
5. **Customizing AI Solutions for Specific Business Needs**
   AI solutions can be tailored to specific industries or business needs. For example, in retail, AI can predict customer preferences and recommend inventory purchases. In finance, AI can automate loan approval processes or provide real-time fraud detection.

Challenge Question:

What specific business area (e.g., pricing, inventory, financial forecasting) do you think could benefit most from AI in your business or industry? What steps would you take to begin integrating AI into this area?

Key Takeaways

- AI offers tremendous advantages in business mathematics, including enhanced data analysis, automation, improved accuracy, and real-time decision-making.
- By strategically integrating AI into financial modeling, inventory management, pricing, and risk assessment, businesses can make more informed, efficient, and proactive decisions.

Discussion Prompt:

Imagine you're the manager of a growing business. How could you use AI to optimize your company's operations? What challenges might you face when adopting AI, and how could you overcome them?

Final Thoughts

AI is transforming the landscape of business mathematics by providing tools that are faster, more accurate, and capable of making real-time decisions. As businesses continue to embrace AI, the potential for creating significant impacts in financial planning, operational efficiency, and strategic decision-making will only grow. Now is the time to explore how AI can elevate your business math processes and drive success.

www.ingramcontent.com/pod-product-compliance
Lightning Source LLC
Chambersburg PA
CBHW070949220526
45471CB00007B/2953

www.ingramcontent.com/pod-product-compliance
Lightning Source LLC
Chambersburg PA
CBHW071002220526
45471CB00007B/3142